# Edmund the Terrible Raccoon

**Canadian Cataloguing in Publication Data**

Duchesne, Christiane, 1949-
[Edmond, l'affreux raton. English]
Edmund the Terrible Raccoon
Translation of: Edmond, l'affreux raton.
For children.

ISBN 1-894363-31-0

I. Beshwaty, Steve. II. Perkes, Carolyn, 1954- .
III.Title. IV. Title: Edmond, l'affreux raton. English.

PS8557.U265E3513 1998   jC843'.54  C98-940987-2
PS9557.U265E3513 1998
PZ7.D82Ed 1998

Publisher: Dominique Payette
English text: Carolyn Perkes
Series Editor: Lucie Papineau

Artistic direction and graphic design:
Diane Primeau

Legal Deposit: 3rd Quarter 1998
National Library of Canada
Bibliothèque nationale du Québec

ISBN 1-894363-31-0

Printed in Canada

10  9  8  7  6  5  4  3

**Dominique & Friends**
A division of Les Éditions Héritage inc.

Canada:
300 Arran Street, Saint-Lambert
Québec, Canada  J4R 1K5

U.S.A.:
P.O. Box 800,
Champlain, New York  12919

Tel.: 1-888-228-1498
Fax: 1-888-782-1481
E-mail: dominique.friends@editionsheritage.com

We wish to thank the Canada Council for the Arts, SODEC
and the Department of Canadian Heritage for assisting our
publications program.

Text: Christiane Duchesne
Illustrations: Steve Beshwaty
English text: Carolyn Perkes

# Edmund the Terrible Raccoon

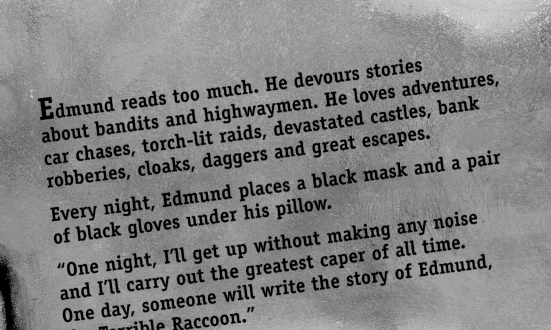

Edmund reads too much. He devours stories about bandits and highwaymen. He loves adventures, car chases, torch-lit raids, devastated castles, bank robberies, cloaks, daggers and great escapes.

Every night, Edmund places a black mask and a pair of black gloves under his pillow.

"One night, I'll get up without making any noise and I'll carry out the greatest caper of all time. One day, someone will write the story of Edmund, the Terrible Raccoon."

Not far from Edmund's house lives Bertha the frog. She is very rich, very mean and very ugly. No one likes Bertha the frog.

"And what if I stole her fortune?" Edmund wonders.

His mother wishes him good night and quietly closes his bedroom door.

"Oh yes!" murmurs Edmund. "Tonight's the night! Bertha the frog, here I come!"

He silently slips on his black gloves, adjusts his mask and grabs a big bag.

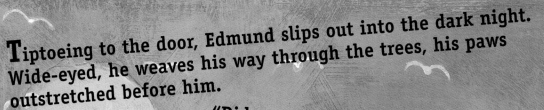

Tiptoeing to the door, Edmund slips out into the dark night.
Wide-eyed, he weaves his way through the trees, his paws
outstretched before him.

"Did you see that?" the owl whispers to her twelve sisters.
"Edmund is sleepwalking!"

"I'm not Edmund!" he bellows, disguising his voice.
"Go home! If you don't, I'll turn you into a shish-kebab!"

Terrified, the thirteen owls fly away into the night.

"A fortune! A fortune all to myself!"
Edmund croons softly.

"Is that you, Edmund?"

"I'm not Edmund," he growls in a deep dark voice.
"Go home! If you don't, I'll chop you up into little pieces!"

"Forgive me, but I can't see very well," stutters the frightened
old mole. "I thought I recognized Edmund's voice."

Edmund crawls to the pond where Bertha the frog lives. Suddenly, the great heron's voice booms overhead.

"Edmund, what are you doing here?" the heron asks sternly.

"I'm not Edmund!"

"I don't believe you," the great bird scoffs. "But whoever you are, you should know better than to disturb the watchful heron."

"Be quiet! Or I'll gobble up your long legs and your big, skinny neck!"

Edmund continues along his way in silence. Finally he reaches Bertha's house. Everything is dark; Bertha must be sleeping. He slips inside without making a sound.

"Is that you, Edmund? I recognized your little raccoon footsteps," says Bertha, from under her blankets.

"Yes, it's me!" Edmund says. "I've come to visit you."

"Oh, how sweet of you!" Bertha answers. "And I was having trouble sleeping. Would you like to tell me a story?"

Edmund leaps into the bedroom, pulls a long rope out of his bag and ties the frog up tightly to the bars of her bed. He tickles the soles of her feet, then he gags her big frog mouth.

Edmund searches under the bed and in the chimney; he ransacks the cupboards and the suitcases hidden at the bottom of the closets. Everywhere he looks, he finds bags filled with gold and silver, jewels, pearls, rare candy and treasures, treasures everywhere in the house. He fills his bag, while Bertha the frog squirms like an eel.

"**I**'m not Edmund, I lied to you!" he declares. "I am the Terrible Raccoon! And the Terrible Raccoon is rich, thanks to you!" he adds with a snicker.

Edmund runs out of the house, the heavy bag slung over his shoulder.

"Edmund? Is that you again?" cries the heron in his husky voice.

Edmund doesn't slow down.

"Edmund! Aren't you sleeping?" whispers the old mole.

Edmund keeps on running.

"Edmund?" call the thirteen owls. "Go to bed, it's very late."

"I am not Edmund!" he cries out to the entire forest. "And I'll have your hides if you open your mouths again!"

"Edmund, is that you?" asks his mother, alerted by the noise.

"I'm not Edmund!" he yells at the top of his lungs. "I am the Terrible Raccoon and I've just stolen the frog's fortune!" Just then, Edmund realizes that he is standing in front of his own house.

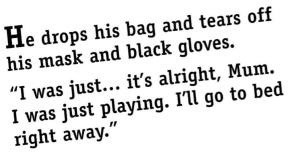

He drops his bag and tears off his mask and black gloves.

"I was just... it's alright, Mum. I was just playing. I'll go to bed right away."

But Edmund's mother has already opened the bag and found her three pearl necklaces and her thirty silver coins, the earrings belonging to the thirteen owls, the old mole's candlesticks, the heron's treasure and all sorts of other things that had disappeared long ago.

"Oh, Edmund!" she cries happily. "So it was Bertha? It was Bertha who stole everything from us? Tomorrow morning, we'll give everything back to the rightful owners. But," she adds, "what have you done with that awful thief?"

"I tied her up."

"Edmund!" his mother scolds.

The next day, the animals come to collect their possessions. Bertha the frog must apologize to the raccoon family, the thirteen owls, the old mole and the great heron, and swear that she'll never steal again. There is a big party for Edmund, with a cake that reads "For Edmund, the Good Raccoon" in dark chocolate letters.

Meanwhile, Edmund dreams of the day when he will read instead:

## For Edmund, the Terrible Raccoon.